INSIDER'S GUIDE TO HOME BUYING
San Francisco Edition

SHAWN KUNKLER

Printed in the United States of America

First Printing, 2017

ISBN: 978-0-9997829-0-3

Kunk & Kunk Publishing
www.shawnkunkler.com

Author photograph by Cielo de la Paz, www.cielod.com, the Storyographist
Cover design by Michael Manganaan of Paragon Real Estate Group
Formatting and layout by Sheenah Freitas of Tokki Book Designs

Disclaimer

Although the information in the Insiders Guide to Home Buying *San Francisco edition* is believed accurate at the time of publication, persons using the information should check for possible changes and other industry developments and trends of more recent date. The author and publisher have made every effort to ensure that the information in this book was correct at time of printing, the author and publisher do not assume and hereby disclaim any liability to any party for any loss, damage, or disruption caused by errors or omissions, whether such errors or omissions result from negligence, accident, or any other cause. This book is intended as a general guide and does not deliver accounting, legal or financial advice. This book is not intended as a substitute for professional advice.

Special thanks

This book is for my Mom who instilled in me that I can do <u>anything</u> I set my mind to. For my Dad who taught me the value of hard, hard work. For Ann-Marie and Vicky who have always given me unconditional love and support. For Gabby who is a wonderful ball of energy and for Maranda whose tenacity helped get this book to print!

For Cielo who keeps me in balance. I appreciate the nourishing soul that you are. For Nolan and Grayson for keeping me young at heart.

In loving memory of my Grandparents. Thank you, Grammie Nellie, for help awakening the entrepreneur within.

TABLE OF CONTENTS

Introduction 1

What Inspires Me to Help 1

A Little Extra 2

One Size Does NOT Fit All 3

Congratulations—You're Buying a Home 3

Understanding the Market 5

Market Trends 5

Sellers Market 5

Neutral Market 6

Buyer's Market 6

Getting the Best Deal 7

What are "Comps" 8

Pricing Strategies Sellers Deploy 8

Too Many Days on the Market (DOM) 9

Building Your Team (Agent/Lender) 10

Don't Go at it Alone 10

Who is on Your Team? 11

Qualities of Your Agent 12

Who Else is on Your Agent's Speed Dial? 13

Do I Really Need a Buying Agent? 14

What Can I Expect From My Agent? 14

How Does The Buyer's Agent Get Paid? 15

Financing **16**
Choosing a Lender 16
Pre-Approved 16
What Can I Really Afford? 17
Common Closing Costs 17
Wire Fraud 17

Property Types **18**
Single Family Home 18
Condominium 19
Tenancy in Common 19
Co-op 20

Know What You Want **21**
What do You Want? 21
You Don't Know What You Don't Know. 21
"For Now Home" vs. "Forever Home" 22
The 70% Rule. 22
Putting it all Together 22
The Worksheet. 24
Must Haves. 24
Why This List will Help Your Agent 25
Before You Jump Too Far Ahead 25
Would you Write an Offer Today?. 25

The Hunt is Afoot. **26**
Online Adventures 26
Google Maps. 26
Open Houses 27
Post Open House Tours. 28
San Francisco's Broker Tour. .28
Private Showings. 28
Grab Statements and Take Notes to Remember. 28
Compare and Contrast 29

Use Your Phone. 29
Deeper Dive 29

Emotions. 31
Meditation 31
Overthinking 32
Cold Feet 32

We Will Take It! 35
Disclosures 35
Learning about the HOA 35
Inspection Reports 36
Inspection Costs 36
Highest and Best. 36
The Love letter 38
Negotiate for a Win. 38

Common Myths 39
Behind the Scenes 39

Final Thoughts 41
Closing 41
Yes, I Will Help. 41
Nice Socks. 42

The Home Buying Flowchart. 44

Moving Checklist 45

About the Author 47

INTRODUCTION

What Inspires Me to Help

I grew up in Connecticut, the youngest of three. I am fortunate enough to have two amazing sisters, an exceptionally hard working Dad and a Mom who has unconditionally loved me even through the mullet years. Little did I know that at the age of five my world would drastically change. My parents divorced, the economy turned and we would have to move. By the time I was a teen we moved 13 times. Thinking back on this chapter it was this experience that shaped my character and drove me to the real estate industry.

Somewhere in my twenties, I decided to explore the world outside New England. This was right around the time the Red Hot Chili Peppers released their smash hit *Californication*. I would like to think of this song as my own little sign from universe because a few months later I found myself living in the place they wrote about. I remember the first day here like it was yesterday. I was strolling down Fillmore Street in Pacific Heights with nothing but blue skies overhead. It was around 90 degrees and my forehead was pink from being kissed by the sun. Unfortunately on day two the fog rolled in and I needed to wear a coat to stay warm as a blanket of gray enveloped the City.

I have not always been incredibly driven. My Kung Fu teacher often said, "if you are not early, you're late." I took this simple lesson way too seriously. I showed up early to every training session and often times before he did. It actually happened so frequently and for so long that one day he just handed me keys to the studio and said, "you should just let yourself in and practice." So that is what I did! What I learned while pursuing my black belt was simple; show up early, show up often and work like hell. The reality is that I was not the fastest, biggest or strongest person in my class or in the school for that matter but I never cared about that. The incantation I chanted in my head was, "I will not be out worked, period." So I showed up early and stayed late. It was that attitude that allowed me to earn a black belt in a short period of time and ultimately catapulted me to becoming the Program Director for the Federation Headquarter School right here in San Francisco. It is this conditioned attitude that I now apply daily to run my business and help clients achieve their home buying goals.

These core experiences, among many others, have influenced who I am. During most of my professional career, I have considered myself a consultant, and a coach. My goal is always to discover strategies to empower others rather than doing the heavy lifting for them. At this point in my career there are few things that are more rewarding than handing a client the keys to their castle.

I firmly believe that the opposite of fun is not work, it's depression. In all sincerity, I absolutely love what I do. When I am not submerged in the world of real estate, you can find me hanging with family, buried in a book, playing with motorcycles, or enjoying some far-off land. My perfect day is one shared with those I appreciate most.

A Little Extra

Thank you Cielo de la Paz from the bottom of my heart for including me in your *follow your passion* YouTube video series, *"A story about Shawn Kunkler, a San Francisco Realtor"*.

More About This Book | One Size Does NOT Fit All

I am a real estate agent. My training, education, and personal experiences have influenced the content of what you are about to read. I did not write a fluff filled one-size-fits-all book. In real estate, as in life, this would not be impossible.

Markets are different from neighborhood to neighborhood and street to street. The San Francisco real-estate scene is exceptionally unique, so the goal of this book is to inform, educate, and inspire. Hopefully even entertain.

That being said, this book is a supplement, not the meal. My advice is to not go at this alone. Do your homework, perform your due diligence and prepare to ask questions.

Congratulations—You're Buying a Home

You are set on buying a home—congratulations! While researching the best topics for this book I read dozens of "how to buy a home" books, guides and websites. Unfortunately, they all fell short. Boring. Dry. Wordy.... Those books and sites spent copious amounts of time selling you on why you should *buy now* rather than supplying you with the base layer of "how to get started" information. So, the goal here was to create a quick, concise, user friendly guide for people mid-step into the home buying process. Check, check and check!

Listen, the home buying process is confusing enough with so much happening all at once. There is absolutely no point in watering anything down or wandering around covering far off "what if" topics. What you hold in your hands is a quick and concise field guide for savvy buyers who do not have time to waste.

Think of this as the straight line A to Z, Cliff Notes version of the initial home buying process. Will it cover all the bases? NO. But it will certainly offer a clear direction to strategically get in front of the competition.

UNDERSTANDING THE MARKET

Market Trends

Housing markets across the US are like snowflakes, no two are 100% alike. This chapter will provide data points to help you best grasp the current housing market. Within cities, we often see hyperlocal markets. In order to buy successfully, take some time to familiarize yourself with these factors. Ask your agent to send you listings. This needs to be comprised of active listings, pending sales, and recently sold properties in neighborhoods you are interested in. Getting familiar with a few different market trends will help you understand what is happening in real time.

Sellers Market

What drives a sellers market?

San Francisco's Silicon Valley in recent years will help explain.

Silicon Valley is home to international brands like Apple, Google, Cisco, Oracle, Tesla, Facebook, and Salesforce to name a few. These companies grow by recruiting the absolute best talent from around the world. Mix that with a finite amount of space, high rents, low interest rates, and desirability are a few additional factors that gained San Francisco's market growth international recognition.

A few signs you may notice during a seller's market:

- Fewer days on market
- Far more buyers than properties available
- Multiple offers
- Competing with all cash buyers
- Reduced/waived contingencies

Neutral Market

The market trend between a hot seller's market and a strong buyer's market is a neutral or balanced market. In other words, there are an equal amount of buyers and sellers. Some of the base indicators of a neutral market are:

- Selling prices are closer to the comps or CMA (described later in this chapter)
- Fewer buyers circling listings
- Longer closing periods
- Time frames, conditions, and expectations are trending back to "normal"
- A boost in inventory

Buyer's Market

The big indicator of a buyer's market is an increase of inventory. Pace also comes into play—things can certainly move slower in this market. Properties will sit a bit longer on the market due to more supply and retracted demand.

Wait! So you are saying that I will have more properties to choose from?
The base indicators of buyer's markets are:

- More properties on the market
- Average days on market (DOM) increases
- Sellers are more willing to negotiate offers
- Offers are more likely to contain inspection, loan, and appraisal contingencies
- Buyers are less likely to settle for a "good enough property"

Getting the Best Deal

"I refuse to pay anything over the asking price because I want a deal."

The truth of the matter is, people will only pay what the market will bear. If the property asking price is set too high, it will sit unsold. If it's set low, it will sell for more than asking.

With all the variables at play, the key question should be: What does getting a "deal" really mean for you? A good deal can depend on:

A. How long do you want to own the property?
B. What is your goal in buying this property?
C. What are your wants, needs and priorities for this purchase?

We know that prices fluctuate, markets shift, and interest rates continue to be a moving target. The better "deal," looks very different to a house flipper than to my Grandparents who lived in the same home for 40 years. For them, a little blip in the market from time to time did not matter as much because they had no desire to sell. For the flipper however, one little dip can destroy profit margins.

Evaluate how long you plan to live in a home. Look at your current dwelling and how long you have lived there along with how long you have lived at your previous residences. According the the National Association of Homebuilders, "the typical buyer of a single-family home can be expected to stay in the home **approximately 13 years** before moving out." For condos in San Francisco, it is around 4 years.

What are "Comps"

CMA is an acronym for Comparative Market Analysis. You may also hear agent refer to these reports as "Comps". These reports estimate a property's value based on similar (size, quality, condition, location etc.) properties that sold within the past 3–6 months. The reports are generated by real estate agents. These reports are valuable because they help you understand the current housing market and trends. The difference between an appraisal and a CMA is that an appraisal is completed by a licensed real estate appraiser while a CMA is created by an agent and is usually less formal.

Pricing Strategies Sellers Deploy

Pricing a property is more about its appeal than its actual value, especially in a unique market like the Bay Area. In order to drive up a property's price, the seller must get the most amount of people excited in the shortest amount of time.

There are three main pricing strategies to sell any home. You can list it **above, at,** or **below** the market trend.

In Connecticut, where I was born and raised, my mother priced her homes close to what they were expected to sell for. Potential buyers knew this and offered below the asking price. The haggling continued until both parties agreed on a number.

In the San Francisco, we do things a little differently. Big shocker, I know . . .

We love the competition of a bidding war. This is inevitable due to the increasing number of buyers in the area. Listing agents price competitive properties about 10%–20% below the expected sale price. While writing this book, my clients wrote a very competitive offer on a property with a list price of $1.595M. The property sold for $2.3M.

Too Many Days on the Market (DOM)

What happens if a property is priced incorrectly, falls out of contract, or has some sort of other challenge that continues to add to its DOM?

If a home sits on the market for multiple weeks and no offers come in, that home starts to turn off buyers. Buyers start to wonder why no one else wants it. In the Bay Area, nine times out of ten, in a healthy market, the stale listings were priced incorrectly, were poorly marketed or a handful of other base factors. The biggest competition in selling a home is another person selling something similar at the same time in the same area. If other homes are comparable on every line item except for asking price, the lower priced, better marketed homes will attract the MOST curiosity. In short, homes that have been sitting a little longer on the market can be a hidden gem. Buyers willing to look at properties that the market has passed over will have an advantage.

BUILDING YOUR TEAM (AGENT/LENDER)

Don't Go at it Alone

A great agent will be a friend, counselor, educator, coach, and more importantly, a long term real estate advisor you can depend on for the rest of your life.

As a buyer, you have every reason to be represented by an agent. From a financial perspective, the seller is paying the commission for both the listing agent and the buying agent.

My clients, Louda and Elizabeth, had a few questions after reading through disclosures and reports for a property they fell in love with. It was about 11:32 PM when my phone rang . . . it happens.

"Shawn stayed up til midnight getting our bid in order and acted as our therapist through the entire process. Honestly, we needed it."

—Louda & Elizabeth

The reality is, that you can probably find all you need on the interwebs, and in my experience nothing beats the human experience. During an overwhelming situation it is good to know you have someone looking out for your best interest.

Who is on Your Team?

As an agent, I want to know about your investment strategies, home goals, and any timelines you have. These are the kinds of things I typically discuss with clients at our first meeting. The more I understand what you care about, the better I can deliver *your* results.

I first met best friends, Joyce and Jina, at an open house. They looked a little overwhelmed and I sensed their apprehension. After shopping around for a home for a few months, they still didn't know where to begin. We ended up hitting it off and scheduled a lunch meeting to see if we would would well together.

At lunch I learned that both, Jina and Joyce, were medical professionals eager to invest in a property. They had a lot of enthusiasm but felt very lost. What they wanted was to feel like they were part of a team; like someone had their back. As I reflect on that first meeting, I realize that it is clients like them that inspired me to write this book.

Buying a home is a contact sport that requires a strong team. It's esti-mated that 150 communications will fly around during one transaction. As an agent, it's my fiduciary duty to protect my clients best interests. I become a consultant, negotiator, project manager, advocate, and part-time counselor. The best agents are available to answer questions and concerns before, during, and after the sale. They treat you like a lifelong client even if it is your only purchase with them. As the buying process begins, the first thing you will want from your agent is a solid list of reputable lenders to start the pre-approval process.

If you haven't guessed, the lender is your second most important team-mate (assuming you are not purchasing with all cash). The lender is going to require various documents for the pre-approval process. Get on this right away! Most agents will not even start showing properties without a pre-approval because it such an important step.

Starting sooner than later will help you manage financial expectations and get your ducks in a row. Nothing is more disheartening than when a client finds a dream home only to discover it's outside their capacity. Getting pre-approved by a lender will allow you to navigate around potential hurdles. The sooner you begin said paperwork, the sooner you'll finish.

*see Chapter 4 for pre-approval documents

Qualities of Your Agent

When I was in my late 20's I bought a loft in Chicago. My (now ex) wife and I flew out on a Friday, cruised around four neighborhoods on Saturday, walked through three lofts on Sunday, and wrote an offer that night.

Knowing what I know now, I would have chosen a different agent. I learned after the fact that he was a part-time agent, who "double ended" the deal.

Double ending is when the agent represents both the seller and the buyer. Can you imagine if the same lawyer were to represent both the plaintiff and defendant in a legal case?

I have personally decided to represent only one side during a transaction. This is my fiduciary agreement with my client, I can then 100% serve one party's best interests, exclusively.

Buying a home can be a stressful. Having a professional, calm, attentive, and knowledgeable agent makes a world of a difference. Having an agent who is available is also key. You should be able to text, call, or email at any point during the process without ever feeling like a bother. The reality is, for a brief period of time, you will be married to your agent. So you best like them. And remember, before you get married, go on a first date.

As you read earlier, I always meet new clients at my office before we view properties together. I make sure that I can sincerely help buyers get what they really want, and if I can not deliver on results, I tell them. Agents, like me, will only work with a few home buyers at any one time. This allows for optimal availability and consistent communication.

You'll only have one agent, so finding the right fit is important. A few things to consider before hiring an agent:

1. Is your agent a City specialist?
2. Are they actively educating you (market reports, home buyers book, vlogs?)
3. Is your agent full time?
4. Do you personally like their communication style?
5. Is real estate a third career? Do they bring previous experience to the table?
6. Did you Google their name? *My personal favorite thing to do
7. Do they have lists of vetted professionals they can share with you?
8. Are they tech savvy?
9. Will they be honest with you, even when you may not want to hear it?
10. Do they work for a reputable local agency?
11. Will they show up for inspections, signings, and walkthroughs?
12. Do they have a black belt in Kung Fu :) ?

"Shawn will never pressure you to bid or to push you into a property that you are not 100% comfortable with. He understands that this is a relationship and he strives hard to nurture and develop it. Shawn is your man—black belt level quality!"
—KEVIN & NANCY

Who Else is on Your Agent's Speed Dial?

Lenders, accountants, financial advisors, home inspectors, general contractors, plumbers, electricians, painters, handymen, landscapers, roofers, foundation engineers and other individuals and companies with a *proven* track record.

Do I Really Need a Buying Agent?

Yes. Here's why: convenience, contacts, and contracts.

1. Convenience. Agents take care of the details.
2. Contacts. One of the biggest assets that a great agent brings to the table is their little black book of names. You will have access to the best lenders and vendors.
3. Contracts. Knowing what documents go to who and when is incredibly important. A fast paced market leaves little to no wiggle room for something to fall through the cracks. A solid agent will anticipate the road ahead to protect buyers from potential situations.

What Can I Expect From My Agent?

- Educate you about current market conditions
- Provide you with a list of reputable lenders
- Offer consultation services throughout the entire process
- Share frequent updates on all criteria matching properties
- Off-market opportunities
- Network within the real estate community on your behalf
- Schedule showings and share open house availability
- Present you with a vetted list of licensed inspectors
- Help you to understand value-add cosmetic upgrades
- Provide experienced counsel when writing an offer
- Aggressively negotiate on your behalf

- Provide a complete file at close of escrow
- Provide you with a moving checklist
- Be available from offer to escrow and beyond

How Does The Buyer's Agent Get Paid?

In most transactions, the seller pays for you to have an agent. The seller does this partly for marketing exposure and partly because they want a professional on the other side of the transaction. Having two licensed agents is more likely to create a quicker and more efficient experience for everyone involved. For the seller this means getting paid and for the buyer, it is being handed the keys to their new home.

FINANCING

Choosing a Lender

Choosing a well-versed local lender is paramount to getting your loan approved. It is not unheard of for problems to arise surrounding the appraisal, loan terms, and financing. Having a local and experienced lender with a proven track record of success can make or break the home buying experience. A trusted agent will have a vetted list of lenders with a proven track record for you to choose from.

Pre-Approved

Having a pre-approval in your hand is like having a passport for your upcoming vacation across the pond. No passport; no fly. No pre-approval; no buy. If you are serious about purchasing DO NOT avoid putting off this step.

Getting pre-approved can take some time depending on how organized you are. If you have all the documents ready to go, the lender can get started right away. I have worked with lenders in the past who had my client pre-approved the next day while others may take a few days. If you are serious about buying, the pre-approval is the most critical initial step.

Here are a few of the common documents you will be asked for. Each lender may vary and may need additional information from you. This list will get you started but it is best to have a conversation with your lender right away.

- 1 month of pay stubs
- 3 months worth of *all* statements—checking, savings, and investment accounts
- Two years of federal tax returns
- Two years of W2s

What Can I Really Afford?

A lender or financial adviser can help you navigate this step. If you prefer a less human approach, a quick google search for a mortgage calculator or a rent vs. buy calculator will do the trick. It's pretty easy to get some broad stroke answers online but talking to a real, live human is preferable.

Common Closing Costs

- Closing Fees of 2–3%: these are generally comprised of appraisal fees, loan fees, and various title fees.

Wire Fraud

Wire Fraud is becoming a growing problem. As simple rule, once escrow opens, the wiring instructions WILL NOT CHANGE, period! Always call your agent or escrow officer before moving *ANY* money because once it's in the thief's hands, it will be gone.

PROPERTY TYPES

San Francisco has gained international notoriety for its intense market growth in recent years. When the prices shot up in the City, people started to leave for less expensive areas. This created a ripple effect. Surrounding areas saw an increase in value. Much like dropping a pebble into a pond, the demand expanded north, east, and south of the City. Within the City, single family home prices rose first, followed by condominiums, and the tenancy in common (TIC) form of ownership.

In this section we will peel back a layer and explain a few basic property types.

Single Family Home

A single family home belongs to you. Since it is not shared with anyone else, you won't need to double check the Covenants, Conditions & Restrictions (CCRs) before painting, pulling carpet or bringing home a new pet. A downside is, if any repair, maintenance, or upkeep is needed, it is up to you to cover the costs.

Condominium

Living in a condominium (condo) can be like living in a nice hotel, where everything outside of your actual living space is taken care of. In many cases, the association will take care of the roof, exterior paint, cleaning, staffing, and the list goes on. This is paid for by a monthly HOA (homeowners association) fee. In addition to covering repairs, most complexes will feature gyms, lounge areas, entertaining spaces, a pool, and other amenities that might not be affordable with a single family home or TIC (tenancy in common.)

Tenancy in Common

These are more commonly referred to as a TIC and are pronounced as 3 individual letters. This property type is a little more complex than the condo. The immediate upside is that a TIC can usually be purchased for 10–20% less than a similarly matching condominium.

The large difference between a condo and TIC is that a condo owner holds title for their individual unit while a TIC owner owns a percent of the undivided property. Each TIC owner's rights are spelled out by a contract called a "Tenancy In Common Agreement." When it comes to taxes, these are shared. The building receives the bill and each TIC owner is responsible for their percentage.

Even though this property type is continuing to grow in popularity, it is often more challenging to get a TIC fractional loan because few lenders offer this specific product. Of those who do lend, they typically require a down payment of 25%, potentially excluding some buyers from this option. To learn more, speak with your agent and ask for a referral of a few locally vetted lenders who will help you better understand your financing options.

Ready for little secret? Two unit TIC buildings, both owner occupied for one year, can begin the condo conversion process as per local regulations at the time when this was published. Buying a TIC for 10%–20% below the condo value, then making the conversion, could prove to be a good investment strategy.

The information shared here only covers the tip of the iceberg about a TIC type of ownership. This property type is a bit more complex and will require better understanding and clarification. There are a few very well known San Francisco lawyers who specialize in this property type and would suggest connecting with them directly to explore further. Ask your Realtor for an outstanding referral.

Co-op

Co-op is short for stock cooperative. These property types tend to be more popular in places like New York City, but San Francisco does have a few. What makes them unique is that the building is owned by cooperative society, business, or enterprise. When you buy a co-op home, you don't technically buy (or own) your property. Instead, you buy shares in a corporation that owns it. Owners are typically responsible for monthly maintenance fees to cover building expenses and upkeep like heat, taxes, hot water, insurance, salaries, and other debt the building carries. Something worth mentioning, a buyer will need to apply then interview with a co-op board to obtain approval to make a purchase and become a co-owner.

KNOW WHAT YOU WANT

What do You Want?

Our tastes change. I am reminded of this fact every time I see my junior high school photo. Even if we find our " perfect home" it is very possible that one day, we won't feel the same. This is why a fresh coat of paint and updates are so popular before sellers put their home on the market. Knowing that the average condo buyer in San Francisco owns for less than 4 years should help take away some commitment stress.

You Don't Know What You Don't Know

I was hosting an open house when I met Mike and Tina. They moved to the South Bay from Brooklyn and were looking to relocate to San Francisco. While talking to them they frantically said, we do not know what we want or where we would like to live.

This sentiment is quite common. So as an agent, I always start with what is known. In this case, I knew that the property we met at was a 2 bedroom 2 bathroom condo that had many modern finishes and an asking price of $1.25M. I also knew it was in a fantastic neighborhood with shops, restaurants, an outdoor space, and a central location near the freeway. Based on what I knew, I recommended a handful of similar properties in different areas of the city. My strategy was less about the properties and more about helping Mike and Tina discover the various neighborhoods of San Francisco. The more we saw, the more they began to know their various likes and dislikes.

"For Now Home" vs. "Forever Home"

The Census Bureau says the average American will live in 11.3 different homes over a lifetime. This raises an important question, "how long do you expect to live in your next home?" Having clarity around this can help alleviate some pressure of having to check off every single box when purchasing.

The 70% Rule

Like the "perfect" mate, finding the "perfect" home can be pretty challenging. Home buying can become especially tricky when trying appease two or more decision makers in the process. No two people are the same or have identical taste. When a property meets 70% of what you are looking for, it is worth doing a deeper dive. The next step is to ask your agent to request disclosures and if an offer date has been set.

Putting it all Together

Think about location. Jot down all the things you want to be around. Think about neighborhoods, entertainment, parks, work, outdoor activities, hobbies, walkability, school districts, freeway access, shuttle routes, public transit and so on.

Think about size. Most all home searches are broken down by bedroom count and bathrooms. How many rooms will you need now and maybe in a few years? Do you need a extra room for an office, a den, a laundry room, storage, or perhaps a "garagemahal" for your car collection?

Think about comforts. Dual sinks in the master bathroom? Granite counters? Fireplaces? Double paned windows? Hardwood flooring? Stainless steel appliances? Open floor plans? Pool? Gym?

Think about quality. Do you want a turn key home that you can move right into? Maybe you would like something that needs a mini facelift? Perhaps you are handy and would like a slightly larger project like a kitchen/bath remodel. Or, are you looking to strip the home down to the studs and start from scratch? Thinking these factors through is best to decide before the shopping process begins.

Shawn is the consummate real estate professional. If you've bid on a property that does not fit your initial profile, he will gently nudge you back between the rails. We bid on one such property during our 4 month process and Shawn warned us on the pitfalls all while also diligently preparing our offer (which was ultimately rejected, fortunately).

—NANCY H.

The Worksheet.

Use the blanks to jot down the 10 items you want the home to have.

Person 1   **Person 2**

1._____   1._____
2._____   2._____
3._____   3._____
4._____   4._____
5._____   5._____
6._____   6._____
7._____   7._____
8._____   8._____
9._____   9._____
10._____   10._____

Must Haves

Now the fun part! Put a star next to the three absolute *must* haves. When you have done this please skip to **Why This List will Help Your Agent**.

Same Page (2 or more people)

Running through this list by yourself is one thing. It's another to match it up with others. Once everyone has chosen their 3, discuss what is important to everyone and why. Continue talking this through until you are able to whittled down the list to 3 communal things that you are looking for in a property.

"A mind is like a parachute. It doesn't work if it is not open."

—Frank Zappa

Why This List will Help Your Agent

As an agent, this list is absolute gold. Within a few minutes of receiving it, I can start hand picking properties to show, same day. This list makes *your* vision clear, allowing us to do what we do best. We obviously won't know how a property makes you feel until you actually see it, but this will most certainly help jump start the process.

Before You Jump Too Far Ahead

Now that you've established what you want, compare it to what is selling. Have your agent send you a list of similar properties that have recently sold. Comb through them carefully. If everything within your budget is a 2 bedroom home and you are expecting 4 bedrooms, then it may be time to make some adjustments. It is often best to calibrate these expectations early because it may end up saving time and some heartache later on.

Would you Write an Offer Today?

Ask yourself, Would you Write an offer today? It is ok if you just started to panic a little because this is a healthy question to ask. Followed by, what would I need to do in order to write an offer today?. This question helps put you in a state of resourcefulness and clarify the specific action items you need to take care of in order to feel comfortable with taking the next step. Buying a home is a process and it is good to know where you currently are so that you can move to where you need to be.

THE HUNT IS AFOOT

Online Adventures

Around 90% of all home searches start online. While the internet can be a wonderful tool, it has also become incredibly cluttered. Realtors use an exclusive little gem called the Multiple Listing Service (MLS). Most all other websites and apps pull their listings from the MLS. While those other platforms are great at uploading the data, they are not always the best at updating it. I cannot tell you how many times I have received a call about an "available" property only to share with my client that it was already in contact. To have direct feed access feel free to visit, http://shawnkunkler. realscout.me/

Google Maps

This is the most underused tool. Google maps allows you to do a virtual "drive by" of a house. More often than not, you can learn something about the property without the hassle of traveling to see it.

Today, my clients found a property and emailed me saying they want to see it. They are moving from their current home because of heavy street traffic and the accompanying road noise. So I went to google maps, typed in the home address of the newly discovered property, and took a screen-shot of the 4 lane street out front. A moment later they replied back saying, let's cross this one off the list. A good agent's goal is to be one step ahead.

Open Houses

Open houses (opens) are a great way to see properties. In the San Francisco Bay Area, the popular open days are Saturday and Sunday, typically from 2pm–4pm. Sometimes you'll hear about twilight tours, typically hosted on a weekday evening after people get out of work.

While visiting, here are a few good questions to ask:

How long have your owners lived here?
(This could give you a sense of how emotionally invested they are in the property.)
Why are they selling?
(This could allude to their motivations)
Do you have an offer date set?
(This could give you a sense of timeframes)

Pro tip: If you **love** the home—take a moment to talk to the agent. The goal here is to be memorable, warm, and friendly. Act interested, but not eager.

At the end of each open house, the listing agent will usually discuss the day's activity with the seller. They will let them know how many people came by and who was interested, and also what their experience with the visitors was like. Remember in a competitive situation the seller gets to choose who they sell to.

Post Open House Tours

Agents do not always tour with their clients. If you head out on your own, a good practice is to shoot your agent a quick email/text after the tour. Let them know what you saw, and your thoughts. Whether you love it, hate it, or are indifferent about a property, feedback will help your agent continue to find the most promising listings.

San Francisco's Broker Tour

On this day of the week, agents get together and preview properties for clients. Agents on top of new inventory will tour 25 properties each week.

Private Showings

This is my personal favorite way to show a property. I will typically set aside time to take my clients to a few properties. With private showings, you can take your time, ask more questions, and really take in the home. Private tours are typically the top choice for my busy and more discerning clients.

Grab Statements and Take Notes to Remember

Open houses are an easy way to see a handful of properties in one fell swoop. *Statements* are the printed marketing pieces about the property. These can be extremely helpful as a comparison tool. Jot notes all over them. These notes will help jog your memory later.

Take an extra minute to assess the:

- Curb appeal
- Location
- Quality
- Condition

Compare and Contrast

Bring your "must have" list and evaluate the property with it in mind. Keep it simple. If the property matches an item on the list, write down a "yes". If not, write down a "no". Next to the "notes", take note of whether there is a possibility for a "yes".

For example, if you really want a white picket fence, but the current fence is brown, this would be a "no/yes" because it is not the way you want it, and with a little paint, it transforms into what you want. Let's say on the other hand that the property is a condo, but you want a single family home, this would be a "no/no".

Use Your Phone

Snapping pictures or shooting a quick video of the home, street, and/or neighborhood is a and easy way to remember special details. Many properties have custom websites and these addresses can be found on the statement. These links are great for sharing with family and friends who are not in the immediate area.

Deeper Dive

Once you have located a property, visited a couple times, and shared with your family (who gave it a big thumbs up,) what do you do next? Evaluate the location, restaurants, activities, parking, how safe it feels, traffic and noise levels. Research Megan's law database, schools, crime statistics, walking scores, and/or any other factors that are important to your decision. It is often worth going back to the property at different times of the day to get a better feel for it. Buyers are always encouraged to perform their own due diligence.

"He researched neighborhoods, organized private tours of homes if I wanted to avoid an open house and is just full of knowledge. I can't thank Shawn enough for all his help."

—CHRISTINE Z.

EMOTIONS

Meditation

When I was a little kid, my Mom took me to a white haired teacher named Mohammed who taught me about the art of meditation. I have been practicing on and off (mostly off) for years, and in my 20's, I picked up martial years as a way to continue my training. These practices have been incredibly useful especially during stressful times in my life. I have always found that when I practice consistently, my life unfolds just a little bit easier.

Buying a home is stressful. In fact, it's considered one of the top three most stressful experiences in life. If you do not have some sort of release valve, you might explode. Being a black belt, I am a huge fan of working out, hitting the gym, or going for a climb. I also love taking my motorcycle up the Coast just to clear my head. Figure out what helps you relax and find your center, and make sure to practice it while going through the home buying experience.

If all else fails, put your feet up and open a bottle of red. I mean after all, we do live near the wine country . . .

Overthinking

I am working with a client now who shared with me that she was going to buy in San Francisco 5 years ago, but at the time the prices were too high. Unfortunately, almost any property she could have purchased back then is now worth more today.

I recently showed her a few properties. Much like Goldilocks, nothing was the ideal fit. The reality is that she is grid locked because of fear. The technical term for this is "paralysis by analysis." Wayne Gretzky said it best, "You miss 100% of the shots you don't take." Unfortunately, this client did not take the shot 5 years ago and still lives in the same apartment today. She lost all those years of paying down a mortgage and building equity, among other things. It is good to be prudent but be careful to not get stuck.

Tip: Shop the market. Get trustworthy advice. Then take your shot.

Cold Feet

Fear comes in many forms and usually stems from a feeling of uncertainty. We all worry about all the unknowns and potential negative outcomes. A good agent helps spot problems before they become problems, and intuitively addresses needs to help manage the home buying process. Let's cover the most common hurdles.

1. Have you strayed too far from your checklist? Committing your wants to paper will help during the final stretch. It's like having a friend that you confide in, in order to help you perform a side-by-side comparison. This will help you make a more practical and less emotional decision.

2. When it comes time to write an offer, a few things have to happen quickly. Vet your lender in advance, shop rates, and get

preapproved. The day you write your offer is not the time to discover whether or not you can stomach the monthly payments.

3. Consider reading and understanding a purchase agreement with your agent before writing your first offer. The more questions you have answered prior to, the less stress the day of.

4. Be familiar with the neighborhood, with commute times, and other specific details. Where is the closest shuttle stop? Can be an important detail, especially if your commute is an hour drivetime to the South Bay. Think these details through as early as possible.

5. Know who you are. Personally, I looked at 3 properties before picking one and writing an offer. Not everyone is like this. Ask yourself, are you the kind of person who can look at 1 property and make a choice or do you need to look at 12 before committing? No answer is wrong here and in the end, do what works for you.

6. Reveal your *why*. I recently reread *Think and Grow Rich* by Napoleon Hill after after attending Tony Robbins' *Unleash the Power Within* (I highly recommend both). The common thread throughout both the seminar and the book, is the reminder to discover your burning desire. Genuinely figure out your *why*. Recently, my clients wanted a little extra room. We toured a great property and once again I heard, "we need a little extra room". After being stumped I decided to unpack this one a little more. During our exchange I discovered that Tommy specifically needed the extra room, not just to spread out but because he is a musician, the "extra room" could double as his studio space. Knowing that, we adjusted our search and looked for a studio space. Now that, my friend, is a very powerful *why*.

7. Even if you found your dream home, you might have buyer's remorse. When it happens, it will suck. It happened to me

when I bought my first place. I remember the wave of fear that washed over me, followed by the thought, "what have I done?"

Buyer remorse is extremely common. If it happens to you, know that you are not alone. In the 50's my Grandparents paid less than $14k for a 3 bedroom home in the heart of New England and I am pretty sure they layed in bed that very first night, wondering if they paid too much.

There are a few points at when these thoughts and feelings are more likely to creep in. The first is right when your offer gets accepted. The thought might be, "did I just overpay?" Next, is when the final inspection contingency is removed. "Did the inspectors miss something?" And the worst comes when you open the door for the first time. "Do I really want to live here?"

It is natural to feel this way. My advice is not to avoid it but rather anticipate this happening and deploy a strategy to intercept it. Perform your due diligence, believe in the data, and trust in yourself.

WE WILL TAKE IT!

Disclosures

Disclosure packets give potential buyers a snapshot of the property. These packets are comprised of required forms and all known conditions to the seller. They might include any inspections performed. Disclosures can highlight areas of concern and buyers are always encouraged to have their own inspections performed.

Learning about the HOA

HOA means Home Owners Association and dues refer to the operating expense to be paid by the unit. In San Francisco any and all properties can be in an association. It's best to ask your agent and learn if the property you are interested is. A few great questions to start with are: What do they cover? How much are they per month? How much are in reserves? Is there any known maintenance scheduled or special assessment required?

Inspection Reports

Knowing what is wrong upfront will offer important insight into the current state of the property and the potential investment it would take to correct it.

A few basic questions to start with are:

What is the condition of the roof, plumbing, electrical, and foundation?
Are there any signs of poor drainage?
Were permits used for any upgrades made?
Are there any special assessments scheduled by the HOA?
Question any and all areas of concern that you may have.

Inspection Costs

Inspections can cost several hundred dollars to several thousand. This depends on how many and of what type are deemed relevant. Each property and unique and buyers are always advised to perform due diligence.

A top notch Realtor will have quality inspectors lined up and ready to call. They will schedule appointments and show up for all inspections.

Highest and Best

Writing an offer in a competitive buyers market is as much an art as it is a science.

In regards to the "science" of the offer, you have the ability to adjust two basic factors: These are the "highest" and "best".

"Highest" refers to the most amount of money a buyer is willing to pay for the property. While "highest" at first glance may sound most appealing, it can however be skewed by the "best". "Best" refers to the terms and conditions of the contract. These are any and all conditions attached to the offer. For example, appraisal contingencies, loan contingencies, inspection contingencies, and the amount of days it takes to close escrow are all part of the terms. In the end, sellers genuinely want to know which buyers are fully committed to the purchase and whose offer is going to have the highest likelihood of a successful close.

Sellers want three things:

The highest amount of money, in the shortest amount of time, with the least amount of risk.

The goal is to try to figure out what is most important to the other party. This is where the "art" comes in.

I helped Rj negotiate the purchase of a beautiful 2 bedroom loft in a very competitive multiple offer situation. His offer was $15,000 *less* than the highest but we made it work. What made the offer more appealing was that he had no appraisal contingency, no loan contingency, 14 day close of escrow with 5 day inspection that was pre-scheduled. The cleaner offer and the quick close, in this case, proved to be worth more than the $15k difference in price for this particular seller.

> **"There are not enough good things to say about Shawn, both professionally and personally. He was a trusted partner during the entire process and someone that I am very thankful that I had by my side."**
>
> —RJ P.

The Love letter

For most, their home is one of the largest investments of their life. It's also a sanctuary, a place of laughter, of tears, and mostly, a place to run around naked. People develop a special connection with their home and do not want just anyone living there. This is where a personal letter to the seller comes in. Writing a heartfelt note to accompany your offer can tip the scale in your favor. In a competitive market where 5 offers are expected to roll in with yours, this personal touch can help make all the difference to help separate you from the pack.

Pro tip: Keep the note brief, two paragraphs at most. Three to four sentence about you, and three to four sentences about why you fell head over in heels in love with the property. Remember, Google is your friend. Try to find something about who you are writing this to. Maybe you were born in the same town, went to the same school, or are long lost cousins? Weave it in and create a human connection.

Negotiate for a Win

Knowing who has the power is always best to know upfront. If you are writing on a highly competitive property and trying to get it accepted, the seller has all the power because they can cherry pick from the lot of buyers. If you are in contract with contingencies, the power shifts back to the buyer. Knowing who has the leverage at any given point is key.

> "Shawn helped facilitate the process, performed negotiations very well, and put me in contact with financial professionals that helped me put together a very competitive offer that ended up being the winning bid."
>
> —MATTHEW S.

COMMON MYTHS

Now for the million dollar question, "What will it sell for?"

The internet is helpful, but has its limitations. The truth is, we are drowning in information and starving for knowledge. We are certainly seeing more and more home estimate sites pop up, but they are not 100% accurate. Sometimes they may even be grossly wrong. No two houses are exactly alike, even when they are the same size and in the same neighborhood. Consider remodels, additions, personalized finishes, and other types of upgrades.

Behind the Scenes

Each week, agents tour properties all over the City. Savvy agents will view 25+ listings each week. Aside from getting a more intimate experience of the homes available, this also gives them facetime with fellow agents. The reality is, agents need other agents to make deals happen for their clients. It is this human touch that gives insight into what a property could potentially sell for. Hearing how many disclosures are out , when the offer date is or discovering how many people are touring the home will offer clues as to where the interest levels are and what a property may sell for. What is obtained from this hightouch human interaction is often more powerful than any data one can find on the internet.

FINAL THOUGHTS

Closing

Thank you for joining me on the home buying adventure. This book took over a year to complete and was derailed more times than I would like to admit. Packing a career into a handful of action items is a pretty intense endeavor. I will reiterate that this is only meant to point folks in the right direction, not steer them through the entire process. I would certainly NOT recommend going at it alone. Hire professionals to help!

Yes, I Will Help

My step-sister Patty pinged me saying, "Hey Shawn . . . my dad has been trying to sell his house for about six months now in Plainville, Connecticut. Following all of your success and drive, I wondered if you could help? I really feel like the team doing it does not have the experience, connections or skill to do it. Any advice you could offer would be awesome. Thank you!!!"

Unfortunately I hear this kind of thing more often than I should. This stressful situation can get out of hand pretty quickly for you and your loved ones. Being a full time agent, I am connected to top agents all around the United States, in fact, anywhere in the world. As a step #1, **call me**.

Part of the client service I provide is knowing the most strategic questions to ask real estate agents in order to highly vett the ideal agent to help with your specific needs. This can range from buying a home, selling a property, or addressing a real estate investment question. Whatever it is, call. More often than not it takes less energy to steer around a problem than it does to dig yourself out of one.

Nice Socks

You have probably noticed my socks all over my social media feed. While I admit it started as a way to stand out, it has evolved into my brand. It is always funny after a talk or when I run into someone at an open house and they blurt out, "Oh hey, what fun socks are you wearing today?" James Bond has his shaken martinis and the silver Aston Martin, so I guess I will corner the market on ostentatious socks. But it is all good . . .

When I was a kid, my Grandparents had a little sign that read, "I complained that I had no shoes until the day I met a man who had no feet." This left an indelible impression on me as a child and is something that I carry with me to this day. My interpretation is that there is no point in complaining about your current situation and better yet, it is our duty to help those not as well off. What started as a snarky fashion statement has transformed into my mission to help others in need. A portion of this book's proceeds will be donated to help thejoyofsox.org Together we can help Joy of Socks provide every homeless person in the United States with a few new pairs of socks every year. For that, thank you for your support!

Yes, I Will Help

Do you have real estate questions? Call me 415.857.4188

THE HOME BUYING FLOWCHART

A. Beginning
   a. Build the consulting Team
      i. Realtor
      ii. Lender
   b. Wants, Needs and Goals
   c. Establishing new home timeline
   d. Financial Parameters, and estimated expenses
B. Putting your Ducks in a row
   a. Pre-approval
   b. Learning Market trends
   c. Research property types, neighborhoods, schools and commute times
C. Boots on the Ground
   a. Receive property updates
   b. Tour properties
   c. Explore all options
   d. Locate desired property
D. The Offer
   a. Request Disclosures through your agent
   b. Carefully review all documents
   c. Review Comps
   d. Navigate best price and terms
   e. Offer ACCEPTED!
E. Escrow
   a. Open Escrow
   b. Receive timeline of events
   c. Deposit Earnest Money
   d. Preliminary Title report
F. Due Diligence
   a. Property Inspections
   b. Appraisal
   c. Review Reports
   d. Removal of Contingencies
G. Final Week
   a. Final walk through
   b. Review and sign documents
   c. Buyer final deposit
   d. Funding loan
H. Closing Day
   a. Recording of deed
   b. Close escrow
   c. Receive keys

** Do the Happy dance

MOVING CHECKLIST

Update Address
- ☐ USPS change of address
- ☐ DMV license
- ☐ Insurance
- ☐ Banks
- ☐ Loans
- ☐ All credit cards
- ☐ Automatic payments
- ☐ Employment
- ☐ Gym
- ☐ Schools
- ☐ Subscriptions
- ☐ Memberships
- ☐ Family & Friends

Cancel, transfer or update
- ☐ House cleaner
- ☐ Internet
- ☐ Phone service
- ☐ Electric
- ☐ Gas
- ☐ Water
- ☐ Garbage
- ☐ Landscaper

Pre-moving day
- ☐ Purge, purge, purge
- ☐ Deep clean home- carpets, furniture and clothing

- ☐ Arrange moving company or reserve truck and/or bribe friends
- ☐ Plan ahead for the special needs of children and pets
- ☐ Plan meals and have plenty of water on hand
- ☐ Schedule house cleaner for both properties
- ☐ Confirm all scheduled appointments
- ☐ Arrange storage unit

Moving day
- ☐ Breathe
- ☐ Have cash available for tips and moving services
- ☐ Transfer jewelry, passports and family heirlooms personally
- ☐ Leave keys, codes and remotes with appropriate party
- ☐ Perform a final walk through of old property

Unpacking
- ☐ Find wine, glasses and corkscrew stat!

ABOUT THE AUTHOR

Shawn Kunkler is a licensed Real Estate Agent with Paragon Real Estate Group in California. Shawn is a contributing writer for the *SFGATE Real Estate Soundoff* editorial column and wrote, "Should I consider a home warranty?" (September 10, 2017), "What advice do you have for someone looking to start a career as a Realtor?" (September 22, 2017), and "What are the benefits and drawbacks of listing a home off-market?" (November 17, 2017). He was guest speaker at Salesforce's Demystifying the Home Buying Process and was guest panelist for Paragon Real Estate Group's Best Ideas and Thoughts of 2017. Shawn is also an accomplished black belt and certified instructor who has been published in *Inside Kung Fu* ("The Perfect Training Partner," May 2010), *Black Belt Magazine* ("Why One Sword is Not Enough," Nov 2011), and is the author of *STING LIKE A MOTHA F'N BEE* (Jan 9, 2015), a snarky martial artist's guide to winning. His writing style consists of a concise delivery of information with just the right amount of humor.